Routes of
Cross-Cultural
Exchange

The
Silk Road

Derek Miller

Cavendish
Square

New York

Published in 2018 by Cavendish Square Publishing, LLC
243 5th Avenue, Suite 136, New York, NY 10016

Library of Congress Cataloging-in-Publication Data

Names: Miller, Derek L., author.
Title: The Silk Road / Derek Miller.
Description: New York : Cavendish Square Publishing, 2018. | Series: Routes
of cross-cultural exchange | Includes bibliographical references and index.
Identifiers: LCCN 2016050018 (print) | LCCN 2016050601 (ebook) | ISBN
9781502626912 (library bound) | ISBN 9781502626776 (E-book)
Subjects: LCSH: Silk Road—History. | Trade routes—Asia—History.
Classification: LCC DS33.1 .M54 2018 (print) | LCC DS33.1 (ebook) | DDC
950—dc23
LC record available at https://lccn.loc.gov/2016050018

Editorial Director: David McNamara
Editor: Caitlyn Miller
Copy Editor: Michele Suchomel-Casey
Associate Art Director: Amy Greenan
Designer: Jessica Nevins
Production Coordinator: Karol Szymczuk
Photo Research: J8 Media

Table of Contents

Introduction / 4
The Silk Road, a Link Between East and West

Chapter 1 / 9
Trade Before the Silk Road

Chapter 2 / 17
Foundations and Explorations

Chapter 3 / 31
Goods and Services

Chapter 4 / 41
The Major Players

Chapter 5 / 55
The Effects of the Silk Road

Chapter 6 / 71
The End of the Silk Road

Glossary / 84
Further Information / 88
Bibliography / 90
Index / 92
About the Author / 96

The Silk Road, a Link Between East and West

Hundreds of years after its end, the Silk Road continues to captivate the human imagination. Images of huge caravans of camels snaking their way through the unforgiving desert appear in movies and books to the present day. Stories of travelers like Marco Polo, who ventured out of the known world along the expansive trade route, have captured generations of readers in the West. His tales of riches beyond the wildest imagination and wondrous, alien things were often ridiculed in Europe since they seemed to be fantasy. His incredulous report of "black stones existing in beds in the mountains, which they dig out and burn like firewood" captures just how strange his descriptions, like that of coal, must have appeared in Europe.

Despite the popularity of the Silk Road in popular culture, it is often misrepresented and misunderstood. A German geographer only coined the term "Silk Road" (or *Seidenstraße*) in 1877. But, in fact, the Silk Road was not a single road

Accommodations were built along the Silk Road to shelter passing caravans.

and it carried many goods other than silk. The Silk Road refers to a network of different trade routes that wound their way between China in the east and Europe in the west. These routes were frequently footpaths, rather than paved roads, and they were subject to constant change as political situations changed along the route. Unlike the magnificent caravans that are often portrayed, real merchants along the Silk Road usually had only a handful of animals. They would travel a relatively short distance before selling their goods in local cities or to the next merchant who would continue the journey. For the first thousand years of the Silk Road's history, there is no evidence that any one person traveled its length from China to Europe. Trade was conducted through a series of middlemen.

Sometimes, the terms "Silk Road sea routes" and "maritime Silk Road" are also used to refer to the trade routes that linked China and Europe via the Indian Ocean. However, these are usually known as the **Spice Routes**, and this book will focus on the overland Silk Road. The Silk Road is one of the world's oldest trade routes. Most famously, it carried silk from China westward and precious metals and stones eastward to China in return. Yet countless other goods also traveled along its length, including horses, paper, glassware, leather, and spices. The riches from this trade shaped human history, and empires grew incredibly wealthy and powerful as a result. The lives of countless people who lived along the trade route also changed: some made their living by engaging in commerce, while others were able to buy luxuries like pepper and silk clothing due to the transportation of these goods over vast distances.

Surprisingly, the most important aspect of the Silk Road was not the goods themselves or the money that was made through trade. It was the transmission of deadly diseases, new technologies, and culture—especially art and religion. The diseases and technologies that the Silk Road carried would alter millions of lives. Empires would fall due to plagues that spread along the Silk Road, and technologies from China, like gunpowder, would change the course of European—and world—history. Today, due to the transmission of artistic styles along the Silk Road, characteristics of ancient Greek art can still be seen in Japanese temples—some 5,500 miles (9,000 kilometers) away.

The longest-lasting impact of the Silk Road was the spread of religion along its routes. Buddhism made its way from its birthplace in Nepal and northern India along the Silk Road to China. From there, it later spread to both Korea and Japan, where it remains a major religion with tens of millions of adherents. Islam also moved along the Silk Road in later centuries. Today, it is the dominant religion in central Asia—including the western reaches of China—due in part to the Muslim travelers who followed the Silk Road east. These thriving religious communities are the result of trade along the Silk Road. In them, it is easy to see how the Silk Road is more than a historical curiosity: it led to the development of the world we live in today.

Chapter 1

Trade Before the Silk Road

The Silk Road was never actually a single road that stretched from the empires and kingdoms of Europe in the West to the Chinese empire in the East. Instead, a series of different roads and footpaths connected important cities along the way. The deserts that presented a major obstacle to caravans were crisscrossed with different routes. Caravans would often converge at the same oasis before taking different routes to the next oasis the following day. Yet there were never huge caravans that traveled the vast distance between Rome and China. Merchants would usually have only a handful of pack animals, and they would travel a tiny portion of the route before selling their goods to the next middleman.

In this way, even at the height of the Silk Road, trade was slow and piecemeal. Goods from China would trade hands many times before arriving in

Opposite: Alexander the Great's armies marched all the way from Europe to India, uniting East and West like never before.

markets in the Middle East and Europe. But before the Silk Road was established in 130 BCE, trade was even slower and more fractured. Archaeologists know that goods from China made their way to Europe hundreds of years before 130 BCE, but China was not trying to promote trade with the West at that time. Goods just naturally moved across borders as people bought them and then resold them over short distances. Nomadic traders also covered great distances and would resell goods they had bought along the way. It was only after 130 BCE that a trade route was established between the East and West. Infrastructure to support trade began to develop: **caravanserai**—inns that provided food and shelter—were built along a network of roads to make travel easier. Empires also began to defend these lucrative routes by building defenses against enemy raiders and patrolling the area for local bandits. Over time, trade increased and the Silk Road began to reshape history.

An Oasis of Jade

The **Tarim Basin**—a huge depression surrounded by tall mountains—is a region in western China with a long history. The high mountains that surround the basin block rain clouds from reaching the area. This means most of the Tarim Basin is composed of the **Taklamakan Desert**, a vast expanse of shifting sand dunes. The word *Taklamakan* literally means "go in and you won't come out" in the local language, and the terrain there is incredibly harsh. The dunes can reach a height of over 650 feet (200 meters) and have buried entire cities when left unchecked. Life in the desert is difficult, but a series of cities sprang up around oases

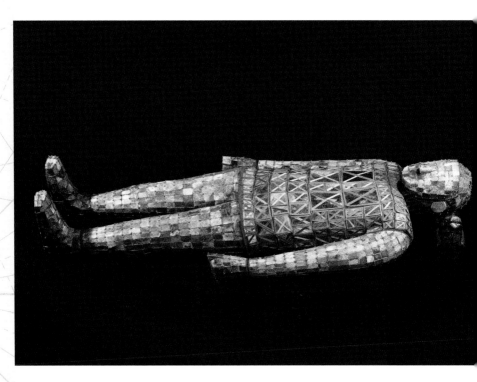

Chinese royalty were sometimes laid to rest in jade burial suits.

along the desert's outskirts in ancient times. These would later play an important role in the Silk Road as shelter for caravans. Long before the Silk Road was opened, the desert town of Khotan was renowned in China for the **jade** it produced.

Jade, a term that actually refers to two different types of rock—nephrite and jadeite—was treasured by the Chinese. Antiquities expert and curator Carol Michaelson states:

> Jade has always occupied a special role in Chinese culture. Its beauty and permanence attracted the inhabitants of ancient China and it started to be carved into ornaments and ceremonial implements around 6000 BC

... Jade's durability and rarity also imbued it with spiritual significance and it was used for religious rites, in burials, and, later, even included as medicine: listed in the imperial pharmacopeia to be ingested in a liquid or powder form. Its durability— and immutability—was believed to confer similar properties on the taker. The most spectacular expression of this belief is seen in the several jade burial suits uncovered in Chinese **Han dynasty** imperial tombs.

Khotan was an extremely important source of jade for China. Every year, glaciers high in the mountains on the southern edge of the Tarim Basin melt in the sun in the summer. This results in a flood of water that comes down from the mountains and passes close to Khotan. The water carries with it jade boulders, and after the rivers stop flooding, these can be easily collected. Jade was also directly mined from the mountains themselves, but the quality of this jade is considered to be lower than jade from the rivers.

Alexander the Great

In 336 BCE, a young man by the name of Alexander became king of Macedonia, a small ancient Greek kingdom. Just twenty years old when he ascended the throne, he would launch a series of military campaigns and conquer most of the known world. Today, he is called Alexander the Great on account of his success on the battlefield. The massive empire that he formed would have a great effect on human history, even though it was short-lived: Alexander died when he

Alexander the Great's empire stretched from Europe in the West to India in the East.

was just thirty-two years old. His infant son was soon murdered, and none of the many generals who tried to unite his empire were successful. Nevertheless, his exploits united the East and West in a way that had never before been seen in human history.

Alexander's army of Greek soldiers marched from ancient Greece, across Persia (modern-day Turkey, Iraq, and Iran), through Egypt, and on to India. The empire he created spread across a distance of some 2,900 miles (4,670 km) west to east—from Europe, across much of Asia, all the way to India. This led to an unprecedented exchange of goods and ideas between the East and the West. Perhaps no kingdom better exemplifies the cultural exchange of the time than the Greco-Bactrian Kingdom of central Asia. After Alexander's death, a Greek general ruled over the kingdom in central Asia and Greek veterans of

Alexander's campaign settled in the kingdom. Their descendants spoke Greek, but some of them practiced Buddhism, and their Greek style of art spread across Asia. It reached even the distant islands of Japan, and today the Japanese wind god closely resembles the wind god of ancient Greece. It is evident that the seeds of cross-cultural exchange had been planted long before trade began along the Silk Road. The start of the Silk Road would prove just how influential trade can be.

The Royal Road

One important precursor to the Silk Road was the Royal Road of Persia. In the fifth century BCE, the Persian king Darius the Great built up the Royal Road from an old network of roads that was utilized earlier in history. The network was used to unite the vast Persian Empire, which stretched across a huge part of Asia at the time, containing the modern countries of Turkey, Iraq, and Iran, among others. Couriers on the road would travel a set distance between outposts and then pass their message on to the next courier with a fresh horse who would continue the journey. This greatly reduced the time it took to deliver messages over large distances. Merchants also used the road to transport goods, and it would be incorporated into the Silk Road once it was established. Today, the Royal Road is perhaps most famous for inspiring the following quotation by ancient Greek historian Herodotus: "Neither snow nor rain nor heat nor gloom of night stays these couriers from the swift completion of their appointed rounds." This is carved into the walls of the James A. Farley Post Office in New York City. Although the United States Postal Service does not have an official motto, this quotation about the Royal Road is often associated with it.

Chapter 2

Foundations and Explorations

U nlike some other famous trade routes, such as the sea route to India or the New World, there is no one explorer who first discovered the Silk Road. Modern humans have inhabited Asia and Europe for tens of thousands of years. Goods slowly made their way through these communities even before the Silk Road became established as a trade route, and during the time of the early Silk Road, it is unlikely that any single person made his or her way across the entire route. While some travelers like Marco Polo did travel all the way from Europe to China, he did so about fifteen hundred years after the beginning of the Silk Road.

In this chapter, we will look at the routes of the Silk Road. The geography of these routes played a large role in the history of the Silk Road and the cultural exchange that took place between the East and West throughout human history. We will also

Opposite: *The Taklamakan Desert. The high mountains that surround the Tarim Basin are visible in the background.*

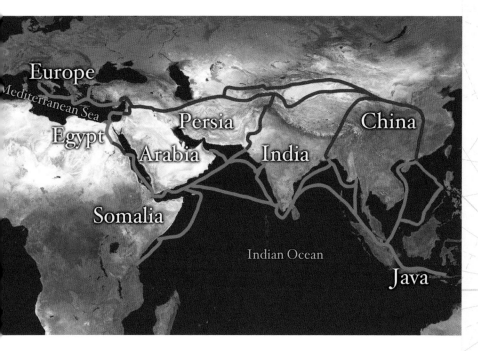

The red path on this map represents the overland Silk Road, while the blue Spice Routes cross the Indian Ocean.

examine the story of Zhang Qian, the Chinese general whose journey west inspired an emperor to turn his gaze westward and seek out new opportunities for trade. Additionally, we will explore the technological developments that made the Silk Road possible, including the wheel and the domestication of camels.

The Geography of the Silk Road

Overland, the Silk Road stretched from China in the east across almost all of Asia to the Mediterranean Sea in the west, where goods would be loaded onto boats to continue their journey to Europe. While the Silk Road was a network of trade routes rather than a single road or route, it was quite restricted in some areas. This is especially true in China. The ancient Chinese capital of Chang'an (now the city of Xian) is usually considered the easternmost city along the Silk Road. From Chang'an, caravans were forced to pass through the narrow Gansu Corridor that linked the heart of the Chinese empire with the Tarim Basin. Today, this corridor is near the center of modern China, but in ancient times it was the western frontier. To the north lay the nomads that often threatened the empire, and to the south rose the natural barrier of the Tibetan Plateau—the highest plateau in the world. Sections of the Great Wall of China were built to defend this vital portion of the Silk Road. At the Tarim Basin, the Silk Road split into the northern and southern routes, depending on which way caravans went to avoid the deadly Taklamakan Desert.

Both the northern and southern routes skirted the high mountains ringing the Tarim Basin and the desert in the middle. By stopping in a number of oasis towns, caravans were able to traverse this inhospitable landscape, but any mistake along the way could spell disaster. Many caravans disappeared at this stage in the journey—lost to either bandits or the unforgiving desert. The northern and southern routes rejoined each other at the city of Kashgar at the western end of the Tarim Basin. From here, they continued on across central Asia (through modern-day Afghanistan and Uzbekistan). A number of cities in this region were famous for their importance to trade at the time, and they developed into diverse cultural centers. For instance, the ancient city of Samarkand was home to thriving communities of Christians, Buddhists, and Jews, as well as **Zoroastrians** and **Manicheans**. The constant influx of different goods and merchants from neighboring countries created a melting pot of cultures. The political landscape of this region changed constantly as nomads and kingdoms clashed repeatedly throughout the centuries and foreign empires managed to exert influence over the region when they were in positions of strength.

From central Asia, the Silk Road continued through the ancient **Near East** (today this region is called the Middle East). This area of the route was usually ruled by one vast empire. At the beginning of the Silk Road, this was the Parthian Empire—a fierce rival of the Roman Empire—but many empires would rise and fall during the sixteen-hundred-year history of the Silk Road. The tendency for this region to be ruled by a large empire meant that merchants could usually travel safely in a stable region on this part of the journey. But the empires guarded the lucrative trade route quite jealously. They often did not allow Roman (and later European) merchants or Chinese merchants to travel through their country. Instead, they took on the role of middlemen in the Silk Road and accumulated vast quantities of wealth as a result.

From this point, goods either continued into modern-day Turkey or were placed onto ships in the Levant (modern-day Syria, Israel, and Lebanon) and transported across the Mediterranean Sea to European cities. Of course, the Silk Road also transported goods from Europe to China following the reverse of this route. As you can imagine, goods traded hands many times during this long and arduous trip across different countries. Many goods were also sold off at cities along the way and never made it all the way to Europe from China.

Maritime Routes

In addition to these overland routes, a vast web of maritime trade routes is sometimes considered part of the Silk Road, although these routes are often referred to as the Spice Routes. These routes crisscrossed a number of seas. To the east, they linked many different islands—such as those of modern-day Indonesia, the Philippines, and Japan—to China. They also provided an alternate route for goods to reach the West by skirting mainland Asia and going around the continent across the seas to the south. The land and sea routes were connected at many points as well. Goods might be carried most of the way to Europe by sea before joining a land caravan for the last part of their journey to the Mediterranean.

War of the Heavenly Horses

Just like its geography, China's history is also complex. Over the course of the past four thousand years, a series of different Chinese empires ruled over an ever-changing territory. At times, China was united and at others it was fractured. But throughout most of Chinese history, there was one constant: conflict with nomadic groups who lived in the steppe—a huge expanse of grassland north of China. The most famous of these nomads is Genghis Khan, who would create one of the largest empires in human history. Yet even before the existence of the Mongol Empire, these nomads were a constant threat to China.

In 139 BCE, China was ruled by Emperor Wudi of the Han dynasty. He had expanded the borders of his empire through a series of wars, but the nomadic Xiongnu Empire to the north of China proved difficult

The Great Wall
of China

The Great Wall of China is famous around the world for its
monumental scale and age. According to one popular myth,
it is the only man-made structure visible from space. In fact,
this is not true. According to Chinese astronaut Yang Liwei,
he did not see the Great Wall when he orbited Earth. Other
astronauts claim that they have seen the Great Wall, but it is
not easy to do so—other man-made objects are much easier
to spot, such as bridges and cities at night. But what makes
the Great Wall so important is its role in history, not whether
or not you can see it from space. Most people know that the
wall was built to defend China from invaders to the north, but
this is only part of the story. The history of the wall stretches
more than two thousand years, and it had a variety of
different functions depending on the time period. Sometimes,
it was meant to defend China from northern invaders, like
the Mongols and Xiongnu. Just as importantly, it was often
used to defend the Silk Road from bandits and robbers inside
of China. In fact, when the Mongols controlled all of China,
they still manned the Great Wall to protect the valuable Silk
Road, despite the fact that they—the northern invaders—were
already south of the wall!

The stone sections of the Great Wall you can see today were mostly built during or after the end of the Silk Road.

to defeat. The Xiongnu constantly raided cities in northern China and undermined the stability of the Chinese empire. Unable to defeat them, Emperor Wudi decided to seek out allies. He had heard that the Xiongnu were also at war with a distant people called the **Yuezhi,** so he sent a trusted general named Zhang Qian to seek them out.

Zhang Qian led a small group of men through Xiongnu territory on a secret mission to find the Yuezhi. Before Zhang Qian could complete his mission, he was captured by the Xiongnu. For ten years, he was their prisoner, although he was treated well and earned the respect of the Xiognu leader. He even married a Xiongnu woman and had children during this time. However, as soon as the opportunity presented itself, he escaped, taking his wife, children, and his few remaining men with him. He continued on his mission to find the Yuezhi. When he finally reached them, they had left their former settlements near the Xiongnu and had no interest in further conflict. Zhang Qian then returned to China, after once again being captured by the Xiongnu. He was held captive for one more year before escaping for the final time.

Although Zhang Qian's mission to find allies against the Xiongnu was a failure, he told the emperor of many exotic goods and locations that had never before been heard of in the imperial court. Most importantly, he reported that people to the west had magnificent horses that dwarfed those available in China. Zhang Qian called them "heavenly horses." These horses captured the imagination of the emperor, who hoped that they might be the key to defeating the mounted Xiongnu soldiers. He sent envoys west to trade for the horses. When this bid failed, he sent armies to subjugate the western kingdoms and acquire the horses by force, leading to the War of the Heavenly Horses. China eventually won this war and gained a number of heavenly horses. Over the coming decades, China would strengthen its control over these kingdoms to its west and defeat the nomads that threatened the trade route. These actions allowed trade to flourish along the newly created Silk Road and began a new era of cross-cultural exchange between the East and West. In this way, Zhang Qian's journey changed history by spurring Chinese interest in western goods.

Nomads

Nomads would play an integral role in the development and history of the Silk Road. Sometimes, they would stand in the way of trade, but other times they

The lush grasslands of the Eurasian Steppe allowed nomads to thrive there.

would make it easier. Over the sixteen-hundred-year history of the Silk Road, countless different nomadic groups would control portions of the trade route at different times. Some groups of nomads would raid the lucrative trade route, while others would guide the caravans across their territory for payment. When the Chinese empire was in a position of strength, it would defend the Silk Road from nomads. But other times, China itself was ruled by nomads, and the Silk Road was also completely under their control. In fact, during the famous travels of Marco Polo along the Silk Road, virtually the entire route was controlled by the grandsons and descendants of Genghis Khan, the great nomadic conqueror.

In the history of the Silk Road, most nomads practiced what we call **nomadic pastoralism**. This means they traveled with their animals and belongings to find new pastures for their livestock. Nomads had different kinds of livestock depending on the terrain, including horses, cattle, sheep, goats, camels, and yaks. Their livestock was absolutely essential to their way of life. Livestock provided them with food in the form of milk and meat, as well as transportation, clothing (from hides and wool), and fuel for fires (in the form of dung). Nomadic pastoralism is still practiced in some areas of central Asia and around the world in diverse cultures. A number of key historical developments made this way of life possible and contributed to the development of the Silk Road.

Domestication of Animals

The first necessary step toward pastoral nomadism was the domestication of animals. Domestication is very different from just capturing or taming a wild animal.

It took place over many generations as humans bred animals that suited their needs. Over time, the animals changed their appearance and behavior as a result of selective breeding. This process is similar to natural selection, the evolutionary process where animals with advantageous traits survive and breed more. In selective breeding, humans choose which traits are advantageous rather than the environment shaping the life span of the animals.

Dogs were the earliest animals to be domesticated, around fifteen thousand years ago—they likely helped early humans hunt prey and guarded them at night. Sheep were the next animal to be domesticated, about ten thousand years ago, and it is at this point that domesticated animals began to provide some humans with food and clothing. This completely reshaped human life at the time, and the domestication of animals and plants would eventually lead to civilization as we know it. For the first time, humans were able to produce large amounts of food in a small area and support the growth of cities. After sheep, cattle and pigs were domesticated in the next few thousand years, and, finally horses were domesticated six thousand years ago.

The Wheel

It is easy to imagine the effect that domesticated animals played in early trade. Before this point, humans had to carry goods themselves. This would have limited trade a great deal and made large-scale transportation impossible. After the domestication of animals, hundreds of pounds of goods could be loaded onto the backs of horses or cattle and transported across vast distances. Even so, the load that an animal can carry on its back is limited. That limitation was surpassed five and a half thousand years ago with the invention of the wheel. A team of two oxen (a term for cattle used as draft animals) can pull a load of thousands of pounds. This ability allowed merchants to move huge quantities of goods through the use of wheeled vehicles and domesticated animals. For this reason, according to scholars E. E. Kuzmina and Victor H. Mair:

> The invention of the wheel is one of the most important discoveries in the history of humankind. For five millennia it has largely determined the evolution of our civilization. The use of wheeled transport considerably increased labor productivity both in farming, where it provided for the delivery of crops from the field, and in livestock herding, where it allowed the herdsmen to follow their cattle in pursuit of new pastures, which resulted in the emergence of nomadic pastoralism. But first and foremost, it furthered the unprecedented expansion of exchange, which in turn promoted cultural contacts between remote regions and accelerated the diffusion of ideas, and consequently led to great historical change.

The Camel

While the domestication of animals was important for the development of pastoral nomadism and civilization in general, one animal is particularly important in the history of the Silk Road: the camel. Bactrian camels (which have two humps) were first domesticated in central Asia around 4,500 years ago. These were the camels that primarily made their way across the Silk Road trade routes, not their smaller one-humped cousins that are known as Arabian camels or dromedaries.

Camels could carry large amounts of goods over the inhospitable terrain of the Tarim Basin. They are capable of traveling 31 miles (50 km) in a single day bearing 440 pounds (200 kilograms). Horses and oxen were unable to carry such large amounts on this grueling journey—the use of carts or other wheeled vehicles was also ruled out because the ever-shifting sands of the desert made roads impossible to maintain. Yet camels were well-suited to the harsh environment: they can survive the extreme high temperatures during the day and the extreme low temperatures at night, as well as go days without drinking any water at all. The fact that they store fat in their humps also allows them to weather difficult journeys more easily and control their body temperature more effectively than other animals. In this way, the domestication of the camel was an essential step in the creation of the Silk Road. Without camels, the caravans that made their way across central Asia would have been impossible. The resilience of the camel as a beast of burden made the caravans possible and resulted in the long history of the Silk Road that connected the world for centuries.

Chapter 3

Goods and Services

Many different goods were traded along the winding network of trade routes known as the Silk Road. The most famous is, of course, silk. But other goods such as paper, leather, precious metals, chemicals, and spices also made their way along the trade route. Different goods were popular during different time periods and along different parts of the long trade route. One similarity among all of these goods was their high cost. The reason for this is simple: it was not profitable to carry inexpensive goods on the long, often dangerous journey across central Asia. Therefore, it was only extremely valuable goods that made the long trip along the Silk Road—cheaper goods such as grain might move small distances along the route but rarely made their way across the entire route.

The majority of the people who lived along the Silk Road made their living by farming or raising

Opposite: *Dyed silk*

animals. On the other hand, the Silk Road did shape the livelihood of some people. Most goods were transported by merchants who owned just a few animals and carried goods a couple hundred miles—a fraction of the total length of the Silk Road. They would buy goods at one place and transport them for weeks or months before selling them to another merchant who moved them farther. Along the way, many goods were sold to consumers long before they could reach distant markets. These merchants also hired numerous locals to help them with their work. They usually needed guides, since the Silk Road was in some parts a series of footpaths and not an easily followed road. At certain times, the merchants may also have needed guards to protect them from bandits along the way (the bandits were sometimes the very same "guards" who needed to be paid one way or another). All in all, the Silk Road increased the level of wealth along its length, as locals profited from the long-distance trade of goods through their lands.

Silk

Silk has a long history. It has been produced by humans for at least five thousand years. It was first cultivated in China, where ancient people domesticated the silkworm and made it more suitable for large-scale silk production. Silkworms are caterpillars of a specific species of moth, *Bombyx mori*. Due to their domestication, silkworms are quite helpless and unable to find food on their own. They rely on humans to feed them leaves, and they favor white mulberry leaves from a tree native to China. The adult moths of the species are also flightless as a result of their domestication. After they are born, silkworms eat leaves for approximately a month. When the silkworms are mature, they spin a cocoon. The cocoon is made out of just one strand of silk that stretches for thousands of feet. This is what is used to make silk fabric.

To protect this strand, the pupa inside is killed by gently heating the cocoon. This allows the silk to be unwrapped carefully rather than torn apart when the moth exits it. Multiple strands from a handful of cocoons are twisted together to form a thread that can then be woven into cloth. This is a time-consuming process, so it meant that silk was quite expensive to produce. At first, only the rich could afford to wear silk garments, but this gradually changed over the centuries as silk production increased. Silk was so important that it was often used as a form of currency inside and outside of China. Taxes in China could be paid in silk, rather than gold or other precious metals, and in Europe some peace treaties between countries provided payments in silk.

Silk was so important in ancient China that it has a mythical story to explain its discovery. It is said that the Chinese empress Si Ling-chi was relaxing in her garden one day when a cocoon fell out of the tree she was sitting under. It fell into the cup of tea she was holding. When she went to pull the cocoon out, the thread unwound—and the secret of how to make silk was discovered. With the support of the emperor, Si Ling-chi perfected the production of silk and China was changed forever.

The secret of how to produce silk was a closely guarded secret for hundreds of years. The Chinese empire realized that it could gain great wealth

The process of silk weaving

if it had a monopoly on silk production. The export of silkworms or mulberries out of China was criminalized. Anyone caught spreading these instruments of silk production could be executed. These efforts to keep this secret were successful at first. While a few Greek and Roman authors wrote about silkworms, other Romans believed that silk grew on trees—they were unaware that silkworms even existed. However, it was only a matter of time before knowledge of silk production spread. At first, the

Roman Attitudes Toward Silk

While what material clothes are made from is hardly a political issue today, silk clothing was a much-debated topic in ancient Rome. The controversy centered on two different issues: the extremely high cost of silk and the fact that it did not modestly cover those who wore it. Many Roman aristocrats and emperors were outraged that large amounts of gold were being sent east to pay for silk clothing. At times, silk was even banned in Rome due to the effect that the silk trade was having on the local economy. Additionally, many conservative Romans thought that silk was eroding the moral foundation of the empire. They believed that it was inappropriate for men to live a life of luxury—evidenced by luxurious silk clothes and cups of solid gold. Yet the most offensive part of silk to Roman conservatives was the appearance of the silk clothing itself. They complained that it was virtually transparent and left little to the imagination. The famed Roman author and politician Seneca the Younger complained bitterly about the popularity of silk clothes. He questioned whether they could even be called clothes, saying, "I can see clothes of silk, if materials that do not hide the body, nor even one's decency, can be called clothes."

secrets of silk production remained in Asia as people in Korea, India, and the Tarim Basin gradually gained access to silkworms.

China still enjoyed a near monopoly on silk that was sent west. In 522 CE, that would change irreversibly. **Justinian I**, the emperor of the **Byzantine Empire**, sent two Christian monks to China on a secret mission. They were to bring back the mysterious worms that were rumored to produce silk. The monks made the arduous journey to China and stayed in the country for some time before they were finally able to secure both silkworms and mulberry seeds. According to tradition, they smuggled these out of the country in hollowed-out walking sticks. This allowed the Byzantine Empire, located at the crossroads of Europe and Asia, to become a major producer of silk. As time went on, the secret of silk production spread from there and eventually reached western Europe. Nevertheless, silk from China was still prized in the West and the Silk Road continued to see large amounts of silk move across it.

Goods That Flowed East

A variety of goods were exchanged for Chinese silk, including precious stones and metals. Jade was carried across the Tarim Basin to China, as it had been before the Silk Road was established. And the Roman Empire sent vast quantities of gold and silver east in exchange for silk. However, most of these metals never made their way all the way to China. Instead, they remained in western and central Asia with the middlemen who traded directly with Rome. Chemicals also made their way along the Silk Road. The most common chemical was ammonium chloride, a substance that can be used to dye fabric and soften leather.

Glass

One good that did travel all the way from the Roman Empire to China was glass. The Romans made glass by combining a special kind of sand and salt and heating the mixture to the temperature of 1100 degrees Fahrenheit (590 degrees Celsius). The Romans used glass to make drinking cups and large vessels. It was

Roman glassware from between the first and fourth centuries CE

a luxury good at the time and extremely expensive. The Chinese made some attempts to produce glass domestically, but before the fifth century CE, they largely relied on the Silk Road to import glass from the West.

Goods That Flowed West

Silk was not the only good that made its way westward. Spices also flowed from the East to the West. Pepper, cinnamon, ginger, and nutmeg from India and islands south of China made their way to Europe. These spices mostly traveled by sea and not by the overland Silk Road. However, they sometimes linked up with caravans on the Silk Road—and they often met at the same ports along the Mediterranean Sea to finish their journey to Europe.

Paper

While silk, precious stones, and spices were much beloved in the ancient world, perhaps the most important good carried along the Silk Road was paper. This writing material that is now so common used to be made only in China. Paper is made out of plant fibers, but it was not until the twelfth century CE that the first paper was made in Europe. Before this time, Europeans were forced to use paper imported from farther east or use less ideal writing materials like parchment (made from animal skin).

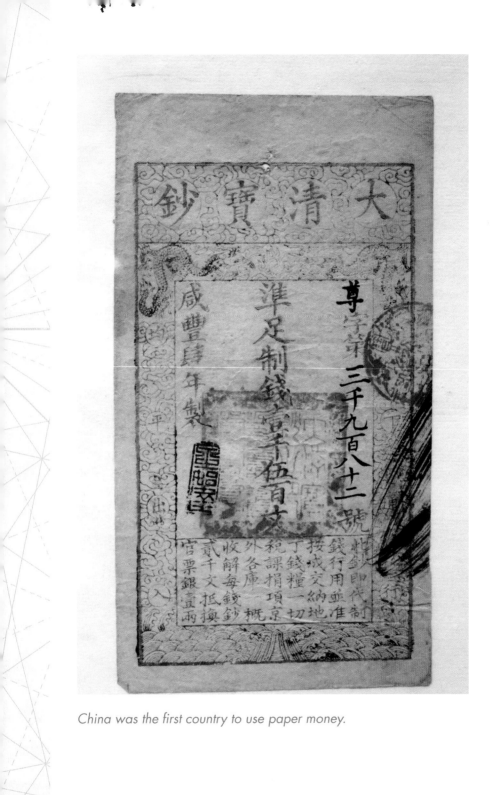

China was the first country to use paper money.

Chapter 4

The Major Players

The history of the Silk Road spans nearly sixteen hundred years. Numerous empires rose and fell during this time period. In the East, China was ruled by a succession of dynasties. In the West, Europe was united under the Roman Empire for a time, before that crumbled and many different countries took its place. Between these eastern and western extremes, a number of different empires ruled the Near East. In this chapter, we will look at the histories and cultures of these diverse countries.

The East: The Chinese and Mongol Empires

China has had numerous dynasties throughout its long history. There have also been periods when no one ruler united the country, such as the Warring States period and the Five Dynasties and Ten

Opposite: The faravahar is an ancient Zoroastrian symbol that is now associated with the country of Iran.

Kingdoms period. But trade along the Silk Road tended to flourish when China was ruled by a strong dynasty that could protect the vulnerable trade route. The Han dynasty, credited with founding the Silk Road, is often regarded as one of the golden ages of Chinese history. It lasted from 206 BCE to 220 CE, and it was the first time that China was unified in a strong, long-lasting state. The period is so important in Chinese history that the largest ethnic group of China is known as the Han.

Culture flourished under the Han dynasty as the arts were encouraged and cultivated. Numerous important works of Chinese literature were written, and entirely new poetic forms were created. Many beautiful bronze and jade sculptures were also created, and intricately woven silk was made both for domestic consumption and export. It was during this time that Buddhism first became influential in China after arriving along the Silk Road.

With the fall of the Han dynasty, China entered a period of fragmentation. This changed in 618 CE with the beginning of the **Tang dynasty**. The Tang dynasty was able to bring order to China and protect the Silk Road. Under the Tang dynasty, the arts flourished, and this period is considered the classical period of Chinese art. Later generations of artists looked to the works of artists during the Tang dynasty for inspiration and sought to emulate their achievements. According to scholar Oliver Wild:

> The art and civilisation of the Silk Road achieved its highest point in the Tang Dynasty. Changan, as the starting point of the route, as well as the capital of the dynasty, developed into one of the largest

and most cosmopolitan cities of the time. By 742 [CE], the population had reached almost two million, and the city itself covered almost the same area as present-day Xian, considerably more than within the present walls of the city. The 754 [CE] census showed that five thousand foreigners lived in the city; Turks, Iranians, Indians and others from along the Road, as well as Japanese, Koreans and Malays from the east.

In 907 CE, the Tang dynasty came to an end, and China once again fragmented into various states that could not unify the country.

Some 250 years later, a boy by the name of Temujin was born in eastern Mongolia. He would grow up to unite the Mongolian tribes and create the largest empire linked by land that the world has ever known: the Mongol Empire. Today, he is better known by the name Genghis Khan, meaning "universal ruler," which he adopted later in life. Genghis Khan conquered a vast territory stretching across much of Asia, and his descendants added China, the Middle East, and even parts of Europe to the Mongol Empire. Their armies were able to defeat forces that vastly outnumbered them through shrewd tactics and the use of horse archers that were able to rain arrows down on the enemy from relative safety.

Genghis Khan and his successors were merciless conquerors. They would usually offer states the chance to pay them tribute and avoid war, but few agreed to these terms. When this offer was refused, the Mongol Empire would lay waste to entire nations,

Ibn Battuta

While everyone studies Christopher Columbus and other famous European explorers in school, few people have heard of the greatest medieval traveler and explorer: Ibn Battuta. Born in Morocco in 1304, Ibn Battuta traveled through much of Africa, the Middle East, central Asia, India, and China. The scope and length of his travels far exceed those of Marco Polo. Ibn Battuta published an account of his travels called *Rihlah* (*Travels*). In it, he describes many places that were on the Silk Road. He is particularly impressed by the riches of China, writing that:

> This is a most extensive country, and abounds in good things (of every description) fruits, agriculture, gold, and silver: and in these it is without a parallel ... Silk is most plentiful among them, for the silkworm is found sticking and feeding upon the trees in all their districts; and hence they make their silk, which is the clothing of the poorest among them. Were it not for the merchants, it would bring no price whatever, and still, a cotton dress will purchase many silken ones.

He is less impressed with much of central Asia, although he does say that Samarkand "is a very large and beautiful city." He traveled through the region more than one hundred years after the conquest of Genghis Khan, but he reports most cities still suffer from their previous devastation during the Mongol conquests, and some still lie completely in ruins with no living inhabitants.

Ibn Battuta

enslave whole cities, and massacre large numbers of people. Scholars estimate the Mongol conquests may have killed up to 10 percent of the entire world's population, or forty million people.

Alternately, the reign of the Mongol Empire created a temporary peace across a huge portion of the world. Although the Mongols were sometimes exceptionally brutal when they conquered new territories, they often ruled with a light touch once an area was under their control. In fact, freedom of religion was common in Mongol lands, unlike many kingdoms of the time. This relative peace led to the flourishing of trade along the Silk Road. And it was at this time that Marco Polo was able to travel across the entire Silk Road in safety—a powerful testament to what has been called the *pax Mongolica* (Latin for "Mongol Peace"), named after the *pax Romana* of early centuries.

Central Asia: The Kushan Empire

The political history of central Asia is extremely complex. Located between China to the east, nomads to the north, and the empires of the Near East to the west, it would change hands repeatedly throughout the history of the Silk Road. Central Asia's position as an important crossroads between empires led to a region of dizzying cultural diversity.

One example of the rich culture of the region is the **Kushan Empire**, which existed between the second century BCE and third century CE. The Yuezhi conquered the region of **Bactria** and created the Kushan Empire. They adopted the Greek alphabet from the remnants of Alexander the Great's army that still

Kushan art portraying the Buddha in a distinctly Greek style

called the region home. Carving out a vast empire in central Asia and northern India, they grew rich off the lucrative Silk Road trade routes that ran through their land. They used this wealth to mint coins and create magnificent works of art that portray Greek, Roman, Buddhist, Hindu, and Iranian myths and deities. They contributed greatly to the transmission of Buddhism into China, and their cultural artifacts remain a unique blend of western and eastern influences.

The Middle East: The Parthians, Sasanians, and Caliphs

The ancient Near East refers to the region that is today called the Middle East. Located between Europe and central Asia, this region was a key area on the Silk Road. It often had close contact with both European powers and Asian powers, and it served as an intermediary that connected the two.

In the third century CE, the Parthians conquered the Near East and created a powerful empire there. Originally a seminomadic group, they soon created a settled empire situated between the Han dynasty and the Roman Empire. They facilitated trade between the two empires despite being bitter rivals of Rome. Over the course of more than two hundred years, Parthia and Rome fought a series of wars. Their conflict only ended in the third century CE, when Parthia fell to the Sasanian Empire: Rome was never able to conquer its rival.

The Parthian Empire was incredibly wealthy due to the trade that passed through it, but for the most part it did not try to expand its territory after its early conquests. Instead, it fought a series of defensive wars against Rome. Nevertheless, Parthia was responsible for one of Rome's greatest military defeats at the Battle of Carrhae. Parthian horse archers were able to outmaneuver the unmounted Romans and annihilate seven Roman legions: twenty thousand Romans died, and ten thousand were captured. Throughout its long history, Rome suffered few military disasters on the same scale.

In 224 CE, the Parthians were defeated by a man named Ardeshir I. He founded the Sasanian Empire, which lasted for some four hundred years. The Sasanian Empire is considered a golden age for Iranian culture. The Sasanians were particularly well known for the silver vessels they created, which were traded across the ancient world. According to scholar Blair

Fowlkes-Child, "As Sasanian culture spread abroad, the imagery and style of Sasanian art left a legacy discernible in the art of early medieval Europe, western central Asia, and China that endured after the fall of the Sasanian dynasty in the mid-seventh century and the growth of Islam."

Ardeshir I established Zoroastrianism as the state religion of the Sasanian Empire. The prophet Zoroaster (also known as Zarathustra) founded the religion in the sixth century BCE. Zoroastrianism is a unique religion that combines elements of monotheism (the belief in a single god) and dualism (the belief in two gods that oppose one another). Zoroastrians believe in one supreme god, Ahura Mazdā, who is good. But they also believe there is an evil being who is in conflict with Ahura Mazdā. The world is seen as a battlefield between the two sides of good and evil. Humans are also a part of the struggle between the sides since free will allows them to commit good or evil acts. Zoroastrianism still exists in small communities today, but the fall of the Sasanian Empire in 651 CE would spell the end of Zoroastrianism as a state religion.

Islam was founded by the prophet Muhammad in the seventh century CE. It spread rapidly from its birthplace in modern-day Saudi Arabia across the Middle East. Less than thirty years after the prophet Muhammad's death, an Islamic empire—the **Umayyad Caliphate**—controlled virtually the entirety of the Middle East. Over the next one hundred years, the Umayyad Caliphate would also spread over most of North Africa and modern-day Spain in Europe. From this point until the end of the Silk Road, a succession of Islamic empires would rule the Middle East. While they were often at conflict with Christian Europe (especially during the time of the Crusades), they also continued to trade with both the East and West.

This period between the eighth century and the thirteenth century CE is now known as the **Islamic Golden Age**. While Europe was mired in the period sometimes referred to as the Dark Ages, the study of philosophy, mathematics, medicine, architecture, science, and the arts was flourishing in the Islamic world. This period of great scientific and cultural advances only ended in 1258 CE, when the Mongols sacked Baghdad, one of the most magnificent cities in the world at the time. The great libraries of Baghdad were emptied and their books thrown into the river. So great was the number of books destroyed that the river reportedly ran black with ink.

The West: The Roman Empire and Medieval Europe

When the Silk Road first became a major trade route in the second century BCE, the Roman Republic was in the midst of a period of rapid expansion. It would soon become the greatest power in Europe, partly due to the conquests of Julius Caesar. Yet Julius Caesar would also bring about the republic's end. In the aftermath of his assassination, it would transform into the Roman Empire, ruled by his grandnephew Augustus.

The importance of Rome in human history is difficult to exaggerate. Romans invented the alphabet we still use today; Spanish, French, Italian, and much of English descended from Latin; republics, including the United States and Canada, were founded on

The Colosseum was built in the first century CE and remains a testament to the power of the Roman Empire.

Rome's example; and Christianity—the largest religion today—spread within the Roman Empire after an early period of persecution.

Rome's power was built on its military and economic strength. It expanded at the expense of its neighbors for hundreds of years, often enslaving the conquered and seizing their wealth. Eventually, the Roman Empire began to crumble. In 285 CE, the emperor Diocletian divided the empire into the Western Roman Empire (with its capital in Rome) and the Eastern Roman Empire (with its capital in Constantinople—at the time called Byzantium). Eventually, the Western Roman Empire began to face mounting pressure from barbarian tribes encroaching on its land. The once mighty Roman legions were no longer the unbeatable force they once were.

In 410 CE, the city of Rome was sacked by barbarians for the first time in over seven hundred years. The end was near, and in 476 CE, the last emperor of the Western Roman Empire was removed from power and an Italian king took his place. The empire in the West had ended, but the Eastern Roman Empire continued. We now call it the Byzantine Empire, although it always thought of itself as simply the Roman Empire (though it no longer controlled the city of Rome for most of its history).

The Byzantine Empire would last for a thousand years after the sacking of Rome. It only fell in 1453 CE—around the same time that the Silk Road came to an end. The Byzantine Empire was quite wealthy, and its reign was marked by a period of scientific progress and a rich culture. It preserved much of the classical learning of ancient Greece and Rome that was lost to medieval western Europe at the time. Although the Byzantine Empire traced its history back to the Roman Empire, the Byzantine Empire was quite different from its western neighbor: it adopted the Greek language rather than the Latin of Rome. Additionally, in 1054 CE the **Great Schism** occurred, and the Catholic faith of western Europe and the Eastern Orthodox faith of the Byzantine Empire split. The Byzantine Empire rejected the religious authority of the pope, and later popes responded by going so far as to declare holy wars against Orthodox countries. Constantinople, one of the greatest Christian cities of Europe, was sacked by a passing crusader army from western Europe in

1204, and the Byzantine Empire never recovered from the blow. It was gradually conquered by the Islamic **Ottoman Empire** until the city of Constantinople fell to the Ottomans in 1453. The city was renamed Istanbul by its new sultan, the name it still has today.

After the fall of the Western Roman Empire in 476 CE, western Europe entered the medieval period, or Middle Ages (between the fall of Rome and the **Renaissance** of the fifteenth century). Numerous kingdoms, both small and large, rose and fell in the power vacuum that resulted from the end of the Western Roman Empire. The borders of western Europe were quite different in this period than they are today: early on barbarian tribes migrated causing political chaos, neither Germany nor Italy were unified, and Spain was soon divided between Christian and Muslim rulers.

Europe was largely ruled by Christian kings, who claimed to rule by divine mandate—or the grace of God. These kingdoms received goods from the East via the Silk Road but were not especially involved in the transportation of goods across Asia. This was usually left to the Byzantine Empire and the merchant republics of Italy. The most famous merchant republic was Venice, although there were others such as Genoa and Amalfi. These Italian city-states were often extremely powerful despite their small size. They relied on lucrative trade routes across the Mediterranean and into Asia to build up vast reserves of wealth and large navies.

Chapter 5

The Effects of the Silk Road

The Silk Road greatly influenced the course of human history. Diseases it carried would bring whole empires to their knees, and technologies that spread from the East into the West, like gunpowder, would reshape the world. However, the furthest-reaching consequences of the Silk Road took place in the realms of religion and culture. The ideas transmitted along the Silk Road would change the way that billions of people came to see themselves and their place in the universe.

Technology and the Silk Road

A number of different technological advances spread via the Silk Road. China was the first country to invent paper, printing, gunpowder, and the compass—sometimes called the **Four Great Inventions** of ancient China. Paper and gunpowder

Opposite: The Japanese wind god Fūjin; the wind bag held over his head and shaggy hair come directly from the wind god of ancient Greece.

are generally accepted to have then made their way from China to Europe. Whether or not the compass traveled from China to Europe is more disputed. And most scholars do not think the Chinese invention of printing played a direct role in **Johannes Gutenberg**'s invention of movable type in Europe (even though moveable type had already been invented in China centuries earlier).

The technology of papermaking spread from China, to the Islamic world, and on to Europe. Paper played a critical role in the Renaissance of Europe, since it allowed books to be printed easily. Gunpowder, too, traveled directly from China to Europe. Invented in China in the ninth century CE, it was first attested to in Europe in the thirteenth century. It was quickly adopted as a weapon of war there, and the use of guns would reshape military history and the history of the world: Europeans used guns to their advantage to conquer vast swathes of the Americas, Asia, and Africa.

The compass was an exceptionally important invention in human history. It is what allowed explorers to discover continents and navigate the vast oceans of the world. It was first invented in China during the Han dynasty—where it consisted of a magnetic needle floating in water. Almost a thousand years later, the compass would appear in Europe, where it was adapted to aid navigation. Whether or not it came from China along the Silk Road (or maritime trade routes) to Europe is still an open question. The fact that the compass seems to have appeared in Europe, before then spreading east into the Islamic world, is often cited as evidence that Europe independently invented the compass: most inventions that came from China were first adopted in the Islamic world and only then made their way to Europe. But other scholars believe there is reason to believe that the European compass was inspired by the Chinese compass.

The invention of printing is one of the most important in human history. Before Gutenberg's printing press, books were too expensive for the majority of people to own. But soon it was possible for everyone to own books, and this would allow ideas to spread quickly across Europe, leading to the Renaissance and eventually to the **Protestant Reformation** that would fundamentally alter Europe. It is undisputed that the earliest printed materials come from China in the form of woodblock printing. This style of printing printed an entire page with a single inked block. Eventually, moveable type—where individual characters or letters on a page can be changed—was invented in China in the eleventh century CE. However, it did not gain traction there since the existence of thousands of Chinese characters (versus dozens of letters) made it impractical. It was only in the fifteenth century that moveable type was used by Gutenberg in Europe and printing on a massive scale became possible. While scholars do not agree on whether or not Gutenberg was influenced by printing in the East, it is unlikely he ever saw evidence of movable type. Perhaps, he saw playing cards that had been printed from a single block—and this may have played a role in his invention. Generally, he is seen as the independent inventor of European-style movable type despite its earlier invention in China.

The Silk Road and the Black Death

In 1347, the Black Death arrived in Europe. A fleet of ships manned by a skeleton crew of infected sailors— many were already dead—docked in Sicily. By the time the shocked authorities could order the ships to leave, it was too late. The disease had spread to Europe, and by the time it had run its course, an estimated 60 percent of Europe's population would die. It would take generations for Europe to recover from the disaster.

Yet this is not the beginning of the story. Most people know that the Black Death, a strain of the bubonic plague, took a terrible toll on Europe. However, fewer people know that it originated in central Asia or China. In 1334, the Black Death struck the Chinese province of Hebei, killing up to 90 percent of the population. From Asia, it gradually spread westward, carried on the Silk Road. It took thirteen years to eventually arrive in Europe, after it devastated the Middle East and central Asia.

While the Black Death is the most famous plague of human history, there were others before it. The Justinian Plague started in 541 CE in the Byzantine Empire (then ruled by Emperor Justinian I). Previously, Justinian had managed to reconquer Italy and Africa after their loss to barbarian invaders. The Byzantine Empire seemed poised to re-create the glorious Roman Empire of old when catastrophe struck. Grain from Egypt, used to feed the massive Byzantine capital of Constantinople, carried plague-infected rats to the city. The resulting outbreak would kill an estimated quarter of the empire's population. This left the Byzantine Empire severely weakened and unable to raise large armies to protect its recent conquests. Neighboring powers took advantage of the situation, and the Byzantine Empire once again began to decline. This plague, too, originated in Asia and spread along the Silk Road to the West. Like the Black Death after it, it would alter European history, upending the political order of the continent.

Art and the Silk Road

The Silk Road would reshape how artists expressed themselves around the world. Artistic styles and **motifs** would make their way along the Silk Road from east to west and west to east. Symbols from across the world would be adopted in distant lands, and a unique blend of eastern and western styles would often result.

One fascinating example of a motif that spans the globe is that of the three hares (animals that resemble large rabbits). The motif consists of three hares running in a circle; the hares each have one ear that is shared with another hare, resulting in

The three hares motif adorning a German cathedral

the appearance of each hare having two ears despite there only being three ears total. The meaning of the motif is unclear, although different cultures likely had different interpretations of it. The earliest occurrence of the motif is on the walls of the **Mogao Caves** in China, dating to the fifth century CE. But from there it spread across central Asia and the Middle East, before arriving in Europe. Now, it can be found in churches across Europe.

Artistic motifs also moved from the West to the East. Ancient Greek art was especially influential, due to the conquests of Alexander the Great and the expansion of Greek rule over much of the Near East and central Asia. The Greek wind god Boreas was always portrayed with shaggy hair and a wind bag raised over his head in artwork. This motif spread all the way to Japan, where even today the Japanese wind god Fujin is depicted with a wind bag held over his head and tussled hair.

Greco-Buddhist Art

While some motifs were adopted and changed by distant cultures, at other times an entirely new artistic tradition sprung up as two different cultures blended together. One example of this is the Greco-Buddhist art that flourished under the Kushan Empire of central Asia. At the time, central Asia was heavily influenced by the Greeks, having been conquered by Alexander the Great. It also had contact with the Roman Empire, and the transmission of Buddhism from India into central Asia was underway. The result was a wholly unique artistic tradition that blended images and religious symbols from both the East and the West.

The Standing Buddha of the Tokyo National Museum

This tradition of Greco-Buddhist art was especially important because it was one of the first instances where the Buddha was portrayed in human form. As a result, even today some Greek and Roman influences can be seen in many images of the Buddha around Asia. One of the earliest representations of the Buddha in human form is the Standing Buddha statue. It is currently housed in the Tokyo National Museum, but it was made in the Kushan Empire and dates to the first or second century CE. The western influences of the work are visible in both the artistic style and the clothing of the statue. The statue's standing posture and young face are reminiscent of the Roman god Apollo, and the figure is depicted in Greek dress rather than the clothing of the Buddha's native northern India.

The Mogao Caves

As we have seen, the Silk Road indirectly affected the arts by leading to the spread of culture and artistic styles. But it also directly inspired art in some cases, such as at the Mogao Caves. The caves lie near the Chinese town of **Dunhuang**, which stood at the crossroads of the northern and southern Silk Roads. It was the last safe stop for Chinese merchants trying to cross the Taklamakan Desert and the first truly Chinese city that merchants from the West arrived at. Dunhuang was also a center of Buddhist culture with a thriving community of monks, scholars, and artists.

The Mogao Caves are a vast complex of caves hewn into solid rock and covered in Buddhist art. An array of colorful paintings and sculptures adorn the caves. Merchants had artists create these masterpieces to bring them good fortune in crossing the desert. The hundreds of caves were expanded and decorated

The interior of one of the Mogao Caves

for a period of some thousand years, and they are remarkably well preserved. Today, they are considered a World Heritage Site by UNESCO, an agency of the United Nations. Hundreds of thousands of tourists visit the site in a remote part of China to see the beautiful Buddhist artwork and a piece of history along the ancient Silk Road.

Religion and the Silk Road

The Silk Road was instrumental in the spread of numerous religions. The earliest religion to spread along the Silk Road was Buddhism. Founded by

Siddhartha Gautama (often simply called the Buddha) in the fifth century BCE, Buddhism predated Christianity by more than four hundred years. It is unique among major religions today in that it stresses salvation (called nirvana) can be achieved in this life rather than only after death. Buddhists believe that through moral action, meditation, and wisdom, humans are able to transcend suffering. Other core Buddhist beliefs include nonviolence and the notion of karma. Karma reflects the idea that past actions sow the seeds of future happiness and suffering—in other words, if one acts with good intentions and does not do evil, happiness is more likely to result.

Today, there are hundreds of millions of Buddhists around the world. Most of them live in Asia, although in recent decades Buddhism has become increasingly popular in the West. But at the time of its founding, Buddhism was observed by a small community of monks and laypeople clustered around the modern-day northern border of India and Nepal. Buddhism gradually spread south through India to the island nation of Sri Lanka and on to Southeast Asia. However, its journey north to China was not so simple. While China and India share a border today, maps do not reveal how difficult it is to cross this terrain. The direct route from India to China is barred by the massive Himalaya Mountains—home to the tallest mountain in the world: Mount Everest.

As a result, Buddhism spread via the Silk Road into China. It was transmitted northwest into central Asia before then spreading east into China. Missionaries and pilgrims made their way along the Silk Road, bringing their faith with them. For a long period of time, Buddhism was the dominant religion of central Asia, although it has since been eclipsed by Islam. In China, the Tang dynasty (618–907 CE) is often considered the period when Buddhism was strongest in China, but even then it coexisted with Confucianism and Taoism. Buddhism declined in China in later years due to intermittent state persecution. Today, less than 20 percent of Chinese people are Buddhist, although they account for half of Buddhists around the world due to China's sizeable population. From China, Buddhism spread to Korea and Japan (the home of Zen Buddhism). The transmission of Buddhism along the Silk Road allowed the faith to flourish in modern times, even after it became virtually extinct in its ancient homelands of India and central Asia.

Buddhism was the first faith to travel along the Silk Road, but it was not the last. Some time between the years of 29 and 33 CE, Jesus of Nazareth was crucified and Christianity began to spread rapidly around the world. While Christianity is sometimes thought of as a European religion, Jesus himself lived and died in Asia. Many early centers of Christianity were in the Middle East and North Africa during a time when much of Europe remained pagan. Most books focus on Christianity's spread westward into Europe, but it also spread eastward—reaching all the way into the heart of Asia along the Silk Road.

As the Roman Empire gradually adopted Christianity over the three centuries following Jesus's death, Christian communities also spread across the Middle East. Many Christians lived under the Parthian and Sasanian Empires, sometimes facing persecution for their beliefs. By the seventh century CE,

Christianity had spread all the way to China as missionaries pressed ever farther eastward. A small number of Christians called China home for the next two hundred years, before a period of religious persecution spelled the end of their community. Christianity fared better in Mongolia, where it became a significant minority religion among the Mongol tribesmen from the seventh century CE until the fourteenth century CE. In fact, when Genghis Khan united the Mongol tribes and conquered much of the world, many of his soldiers were practicing Christians. When the Mongols sacked Baghdad—ending the Islamic Golden Age—the Mongols spared the Christian inhabitants of city after telling them to flee inside of their churches. Eventually, however, many Mongols would adopt Islam, and when the Mongol Empire finally fell apart in the fourteenth century CE, Christianity would no longer be a major religion in the eastern reaches of Asia.

During the same time as Christianity, Manichaeism also spread along the Silk Road and became a major faith in the Middle East. While it is extinct today, it was influential at the time. The prophet Mani founded the religion in the third century CE. He was influenced by a number of religions at that time, including Christianity, Zoroastrianism, and Buddhism. These influences reveal the rich and diverse religious atmosphere of that time, as the Silk Road brought many cultural traditions into contact with one another. Manichaeism spread all the way into both Europe and China, but it was fiercely persecuted in both and eventually became extinct.

The final major religion to spread via the Silk Road was Islam. In the centuries after the prophet

Muhammad's death, the Umayyad Caliphate would rapidly expand over large areas of the globe, bringing Islam with it. People in these regions began to convert to this new faith, and gradually the Middle East became largely Islamic. Merchants and missionaries also followed the Silk Road and brought Islam into central Asia and the Tarim Basin, where it became the dominant faith as it displaced Buddhism, Manichaeism, and Christianity. Today, Islam is still the majority faith throughout the modern-day countries of central Asia, such as Afghanistan and Uzbekistan. Additionally, most Uyghurs practice Islam and reside in western China, around the Tarim Basin. This fact means that the largest region of China, Xinjiang, actually has a Muslim majority due to the effects of the Silk Road.

The Jewish Community of China

The Silk Road was also important to the spread of Judaism. As early as the Han dynasty, there is evidence that Jewish communities could be found in western China near the Tarim Basin. They likely engaged in trade along that important span of the Silk Road. Later in history, there was a large Jewish community in the heart of China: Marco Polo, as well as later travelers, reported that Jews lived in the capital of Chang'an. In fact, there is still a small Jewish community known as the Kaifeng Jews in the city of Kaifeng, once the capital of China. The early history of this community is shrouded in mystery, but it is clear they have lived there for over seven hundred years. It is likely that they first came to China along the Silk Road, the maritime trade routes along the Indian Ocean, or a combination of the two.

The Kaifeng Jewish community garners attention because of its improbability: a Jewish community hidden in the interior of China for hundreds of years. But, unlike faiths such as Christianity and Islam, there is no strong tradition of missionary outreach within Judaism. Thus, the Jewish communities of China simply lived their lives without trying to convert other people to their faith. Therefore, their existence did not radically alter the social fabric of China (or bring them into conflict with the Chinese as many missionaries would find themselves later in history).

Marco Polo

The most famous European to venture down the Silk Road was Marco Polo. He was born in 1254 CE in the Italian city of Venice, and he spent much of his life traveling around Asia with his father and uncle, who were merchants. At the time, most of the Silk Road was controlled by the Mongols, and Marco Polo claimed to have become a member of Kublai Khan's inner circle in China—although scholars still dispute whether this is likely. While Marco Polo was not the first European to travel to Asia, he dictated a book about his travels and this is what led to his great fame. Throughout history, people have debated whether his tales were fact or fantasy. During his own lifetime, many Europeans found his accounts difficult to believe, but many of his claims have been substantiated by historical research. Regardless of how close to the truth his book is, it had a large impact on history. According to scholars Fosco Maraini and Edward Peters:

> Polo's account opened new vistas to the European mind, and as Western horizons expanded, Polo's influence grew as well. His description of Japan set a definite goal for Christopher Columbus in his journey in 1492, while his detailed localizations of spices encouraged Western merchants to seek out these areas and break the age-old Arab trading monopoly. The wealth of new geographic information recorded by Polo was widely used in the late fifteenth and the sixteenth centuries, during the age of the great European voyages of discovery and conquest.

Chapter 6

The End of the Silk Road

The Silk Road came to an end in the fifteenth century. While overland trade across central Asia continued to some extent, it never again matched the golden eras under the Han and Tang dynasties or the Mongol Empire. Different historians credit a number of events with the final end of the Silk Road. But the most important events were China's new policy of isolationism, the increase of maritime (rather than overland) trade, and the rise of the Ottoman Empire, which upset the Silk Road trade route in the Middle East.

An Isolationist China

The **Ming dynasty** ruled China from 1368 to 1644 CE. It replaced the earlier Mongol Yuan dynasty, founded by Kublai Khan, which ruled China for nearly a century. For a time, the Ming

Opposite: Europe's desire for spices spurred exploration.

Zheng He's ships were much larger than their European counterparts during the same era, although they never encountered one another.

dynasty was quite open to foreign trade. The famous Chinese admiral Zheng He lived during the period of the early Ming dynasty. He led a fleet of large Chinese ships on a series of voyages, stopping in the islands that supplied spices to most of the world, as well as Thailand, India, the Middle East, and even Africa. His expeditions were a show of Chinese might, rather than an attempt to establish new trade routes. Yet they led to increased trade in the region as he sold Chinese goods and foreign countries sent tribute to China. However, in 1443, Zheng He died and the Chinese emperor forbid further voyages. China was faced by the growing threats at home, and the treasury was needed to reinforce the Great Wall rather than fund expeditions abroad.

The Ming dynasty became increasingly isolationist at the end of the fifteenth century. All international maritime trade was banned by imperial edict, although smuggling still took place along China's long coasts and borders. The Ming dynasty also came into conflict with the inhabitants of the Tarim Basin. The Ming dynasty eventually forbid all trade along the northern Silk Road in order to pressure its enemies. This essentially led to the end of the Silk Road as a trade route between Europe and China. When the Chinese embargo finally ceased, most Asian goods were already flowing west via the maritime Spice Routes, and the overland Silk Road never again became a major trade route.

The Rise of the Spice Routes

Even before the Ming dynasty cut off trade to the West, the Silk Road was in decline. One major reason for this was the improvements of maritime transportation over the centuries. At the beginning of the Silk Road's history, its overland route was the safest and most economical option to transport goods from the spice-producing islands of Asia to

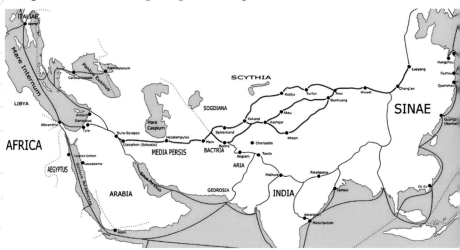

The maritime Spice Routes gradually eclipsed the overland Silk Road.

Europe, despite the fact that is was plagued by bandits and treacherous terrain. At that time, ships were quite small and at the sea's mercy. By the fifteenth century, this was no longer the case. Shipbuilding and navigation had improved to the point that the maritime trade routes were considered safer than the overland Silk Road. Additionally, European silk production had made Chinese silk less important, so the goods that Europe desired, primarily spices, came from islands more suited to maritime trade.

The maritime Spice Routes were a complex network of trade routes that linked many different cities together. Some of the most important stops in this network were the so-called Spice Islands (located in modern-day Indonesia), cities on the coast of India, the Middle East, and even East Africa. Goods from these diverse lands would usually arrive in Egypt, where they would proceed overland for a short distance before once again being loaded onto ships and entering the Mediterranean Sea to arrive in Europe. After the fall of Constantinople, these Spice Routes would play a critical role in the discovery of the New World.

The Fall of Constantinople

The Ottoman Empire helped shape world history for six hundred years, from its beginning in the fifteenth century to its end in the twentieth. It was often seen as an Islamic threat by the Christian countries of Europe since it controlled a vast area of southern Europe and threatened to conquer even more. In 1529, it even laid siege to the Austrian city of Vienna, and the Ottoman armies were only turned back by a coalition of many Christian countries that sought to

Ottoman cannons played a crucial part in the fall of Constantinople.

protect Europe from the ever-expanding empire to its east. This marked a turning point in its history, as it never regained the same level of military supremacy. By the nineteenth century, it was regarded as "the sick man of Europe"—a crumbling empire unable to assert control over its territory. But the Ottoman Empire lasted until the beginning of the twentieth century. On the losing side at the end of World War I, it was dismantled by the victorious powers: the Republic of Turkey is its modern successor.

One of the most important dates in the history of the Ottoman Empire—and world history—is May 29, 1453, the day that the twenty-one-year-old Ottoman sultan Mehmed the Conqueror seized the city of Constantinople. The ancient city had been the capital of the Byzantine Empire for more than a thousand years. It was one of the most magnificent cities in the world, a center of culture and learning, and the last great Christian city in a region that had gradually been conquered by Islamic countries. The fall of Constantinople was a turning point in world history: the era of the Roman Empire came to final close with the destruction of the Byzantine Empire, which always considered itself to be the Roman Empire. The last Roman emperor was cut down by Ottoman soldiers defending the walls of the city against overwhelming odds. This day also marked the beginning of the Ottoman Empire's meteoric rise into one of the most powerful countries on Earth. With the fall of Constantinople, the way to Europe lay open, and southeast Europe would soon be conquered.

The fall of Constantinople was also important to the end of the Silk Road. It marked the end of the stable overland trade route between Europe and China through the Byzantine Empire situated between them. While the Ottoman Empire would allow trade to flow through it, it was often taxed quite heavily, and sometimes it would cut the flow of goods, most importantly spices, to Christian Europe when relations deteriorated. This meant that spices from Asia, like pepper, could only reach Europe by following the maritime Spice Routes through the Indian Ocean and passing through Egypt. However, the rulers of Egypt took advantage of their monopoly on the spice trade by raising the taxes on spices destined for Europe. This would have an unintended consequence: the European **Age of Exploration**.

The Age of Exploration

Portugal, at the western end of Europe, suffered from the Egyptian monopoly on trade with the East. Egypt mostly traded with Venice, cutting Portugal out of any profits. As a result, Portugal looked south rather than east to find new opportunities for trade. During the fifteenth century, Portugal spearheaded exploration around the coast of Africa. Portuguese traders brought back ivory and salt from Africa to European markets. They continued to go farther south, until eventually the famed Portuguese explorer Bartolomeu Dias reached the Cape of Good Hope, at the southern tip of Africa, in 1488. This would change the course of history.

Up until this point, all trade between the far reaches of Asia and Europe had to cross the Middle East overland at some point. Goods either followed the Silk Road and traveled overland most of the way, or they followed the maritime trade routes and passed overland for a short distance in Egypt or some other part of the Middle East. At the end of the fifteenth century, that would change once and for all. The Portuguese navigator Vasco da Gama would sail around the continent of Africa all the way to India and return

A painting of Vasco da Gama's arrival in India

to Europe. Of the 170 crew members he departed with, only 55 survived the two-year voyage. But he had broken the Egyptian monopoly on the spice trade and changed the world forever.

The Portuguese efforts to reach India by sea inspired Spain to attempt the same feat. Rather than sail south around Africa, Spanish explorers sailed west, hoping to cross the Atlantic Ocean and arrive directly in Asia. When Christopher Columbus first made landfall in the Bahamas and then the islands of the Caribbean, he thought he had found India. This is why Native Americans were referred to as "Indians" in the past. However, the Spanish soon realized they had not arrived in India and that their way to Asia was blocked by a "New World"—the Americas.

In this way, the closing of the Silk Road and the rise of the Spice Routes led to the Age of Exploration in Europe. The race to find a new way to access the valuable spice markets of Asia led to the discovery of the Americas by Europeans and new exploration around the African continent. This, in turn, would radically alter world history. European powers began to colonize the New World, transport enslaved people from Africa to work in their colonies, and eventually carve up the entire continent of Africa and exploit its resources. Asia, too, would suffer much from direct contact with the Europeans. Beginning in the nineteenth century, European countries would begin creating spheres of influence in China, demanding concessions (such as the British rule of Hong Kong), and humiliating the Chinese emperors. This is the time period when the Opium Wars were fought: Great Britain forced the Chinese to legalize the drug opium so that Britain could profit from its trade.

The Age of Exploration would lead to European colonization and its many crimes against the peoples of the Americas, Africa, and Asia, but it would also lead to a new, interconnected world. For the first time, humanity began to be aware of the entirety of the globe and the many diverse people who inhabited it. The Age of Exploration set the stage for the modern era where people around the globe are connected to one another through technology and high-speed transportation.

The Artery Between the East and West

When different cultures come into contact with one another, it enriches the cultural heritage of the world. New, unique artistic styles often develop as different traditions meld, and technologies are often shared, sometimes leading to new innovations that change daily life. The Silk Road was one of the most important routes of cultural exchange in the history of the world. It lasted for around sixteen hundred years, and it was a vital artery between the civilizations of Europe and those of Asia. The world as we know it was created as a result of the Silk Road. Technologies that were absolutely essential to world history, like gunpowder and paper production, traveled along its length, changing the world as they went. The diseases that influenced history and ended whole empires also spread via the Silk Road. Trade itself along the Silk Road also shaped the world, enriching some empires and changing the social fabric of whole regions as people worked to profit from the lucrative trade.

The effects of the Silk Road are still apparent in the world today. The rich, diverse artistic traditions that the Silk Road created form key achievements in the history of art. The early Greco-Buddhist statues of the Buddha still influence artistic representations of the Buddha to this day. And the exchange of different artistic motifs from the East to the West and the West to the East left marks in the artistic traditions of both Europe and Asia. The religions of the modern world were also influenced by the Silk Road. Trade allowed Buddhism to spread into eastern Asia, where it remains a vital part of the Chinese, Korean, and Japanese societies. Christianity, Judaism, Islam, and many other smaller religions also found their way across large distances due to their diffusion along the Silk Road.

The world today is growing smaller and smaller due to the power of technology. In the past, people could live their whole lives in a small community. Now, we often interact with people outside our city, and even our country, on a daily basis using the internet and social media. In this ever-more-connected world, the Silk Road is an important reminder of the power of cross-cultural exchange. Communicating with people who see the world differently from ourselves is an opportunity—and not something to be feared. People from different cultures have much to learn from one another, and their interaction can lead to unique insights and artistic expressions. The history of the Silk Road is a powerful testament to this fact, and its example is an important one for the modern world we live in today.

Yo-Yo Ma (center) plays with the Silk Road Ensemble.

The Silk Road Ensemble

Yo-Yo Ma is a world-renowned cellist. He was a child prodigy, performing from the age of five, and studied music at the Julliard School in New York City. Throughout his career, Yo-Yo Ma has been interested in using music as a means to communicate across cultures. To this end, he established Silkroad. The Silkroad website describes its mission in the following way:

> Inspired by the exchange of ideas and traditions along the historical Silk Road, cellist Yo-Yo Ma established

Silkroad in 1998 to explore how the arts can advance global understanding.

Silkroad works to connect the world through the arts, focusing its efforts in three areas: musical performance, learning programs, and cultural entrepreneurship.

Since 2000, the musicians of the Silk Road Ensemble have been central to Silkroad's mission. Under the artistic direction of Yo-Yo Ma and representing a global array of cultures, the Ensemble models new forms of cultural exchange through performances, workshops, and residencies. The artists of the Ensemble draw on the rich tapestry of traditions from around the world that make up our many-layered contemporary identities, weaving together the foreign and familiar to create a new musical language.

Even today, the Silk Road's long history of rich cultural exchange is recognized in popular culture.

*G*lossary

Age of Exploration The era of European exploration of the Americas, Africa, and Asia that began in the fifteenth century.

Bactria An ancient central Asian region that lies in modern-day Afghanistan, Uzbekistan, and Tajikistan; the Greco-Bactrian kingdom takes its name from the region.

Byzantine Empire The successor of the Eastern Roman Empire.

caravanserai Inns along trade routes that catered to passing caravans.

Dunhuang An important Chinese town on the Silk Road at the edge of the Tarim Basin.

Four Great Inventions Four Chinese inventions that changed world history: the compass, gunpowder, papermaking, and printing.

Great Schism The splitting of the Catholic Church and Eastern Orthodox Church, which took place in 1054 CE.

Han dynasty The Chinese dynasty that united the country between 206 BCE and 220 CE; the Silk Road was established under its rule.

Islamic Golden Age A golden era between the eighth and thirteenth centuries when culture and science flourished in the Muslim world.

jade A kind of ornamental stone that is usually green in color.

Johannes Gutenberg The inventor of the European printing press with moveable type; he lived between 1398 and 1468.

Justinian I The Byzantine emperor credited with stealing the secret of silk production from China and whose name became synonymous with the great plague of the time.

Kushan Empire A diverse empire that existed between the second century BCE and third century CE; it was an important creator of Greco-Buddhist art.

Manicheans Adherents of the ancient religion of Manichaeism, which saw the world as the battlefield between good and evil.

Ming dynasty The Chinese dynasty that ruled between 1368 and 1644 CE; its rule was marked by many cultural developments and the reinforcing of the Great Wall, but also the end of the Silk Road.

Mogao Caves A complex of caves filled with Buddhist art near the town of Dunhuang on the Silk Road.

motifs Recurring images or ideas in a work of art or genre of art.

Near East The term for the Middle East in the study of ancient history.

nomadic pastoralism The way of life whereby people travel with their animals to new pastures for them to graze on.

Ottoman Empire The Islamic empire that ended the Byzantine Empire and remained a regional power for centuries.

Protestant Reformation A series of events in the sixteenth century that split the Catholic Church and led to the creation of many Protestant faiths that exist to this day.

Renaissance The resurgence of Classical learning (from ancient Greece and Rome) that occurred in Europe between the fourteenth and seventeenth centuries.

Spice Routes The network of maritime trade routes that linked the East and West through the Indian Ocean.

Taklamakan Desert The large desert that takes up much of the Tarim Basin and was skirted by caravans following the Silk Road.

Tang dynasty The Chinese dynasty that lasted from 618 to 907 CE; Chinese culture thrived under its rule, and the Silk Road entered a golden era.

Tarim Basin A geographic region in modern-day western China that was an important section of the Silk Road; it is where caravans chose to follow either the northern or southern branch of the Silk Road to avoid the Taklamakan Desert.

Umayyad Caliphate The first Muslim dynasty; it greatly expanded the size of the new Islamic caliphate in the seventh and eighth centuries.

Yuezhi An ancient people who came into conflict with the Xiongnu and later conquered the region of Bactria and founded the Kushan Empire.

Zoroastrians Followers of the Zoroastrian religion, an ancient Iranian religion that believes in one god and still exists to this day.

Further Information

Websites

Interactive Map of the Silk Road
http://en.unesco.org/silkroad/network-silk-road-cities-map-app/en
UNESCO provides an interactive map with information about and pictures of the cities that lined the Silk Road.

Monks and Merchants
http://sites.asiasociety.org/arts/monksandmerchants/
The Asia Society maintains this website that describes the history of the Silk Road and is complete with many pictures of ancient art.

Secrets of the Silk Road
http://www.penn.museum/silkroad/exhibit_intro.php
The Penn Museum's exhibit about the Silk Road is available online and includes many interesting facts and images about archaeological finds in the Tarim Basin.

Silk Road Seattle
http://depts.washington.edu/silkroad/
This website from the University of Washington gives comprehensive information about a variety of topics tied to the Silk Road.

Books

Hopkirk, Peter. *Foreign Devils on the Silk Road*. Amherst, MA: The University of Massachusetts Press, 1984.

Liu, Xinru. *The Silk Road in World History*. Oxford, UK: Oxford University Press, 2010.

Millward, James A. *The Silk Road: A Very Short Introduction*. Oxford, UK: Oxford University Press, 2013.

Whitfield, Susan. *Life Along the Silk Road*. Berkeley, CA: University of California Press, 1999.

Videos

"The Silk Road: Connecting the Ancient World through Trade"
http://ed.ted.com/lessons/the-silk-road-history-s-first-world-wide-web-shannon-harris-castelo
Shannon Harris Castelo gives a short introduction to the Silk Road in this video.

"Silk Road Virtual Tour"
https://www.youtube.com/watch?v=56IzyMfLJFA
Dr. Clayton Brown takes viewers on a tour of the Silk Road.

$\mathscr{B}$ibliography

Adam, David. "Can You See the Great Wall of China from Space?" *Guardian*, October 23, 2003. https://www.theguardian.com/science/2003/oct/23/thisweekssciencequestions.

Addis, Cameron. "Age of Exploration." *History Hub*. Retrieved October 15, 2016. http://sites.austincc.edu/caddis/age-of-exploration.

Barber, Elizabeth Wayland. *Prehistoric Textiles: The Development of Cloth in the Neolithic and Bronze Ages with Special Reference to the Aegean*. Princeton, NJ: Princeton University Press, 1992.

CDC. "Plague: History." Retrieved October 15, 2016. http://www.cdc.gov/plague/history/.

Fishbane, Matthew. "China's Ancient Jewish Enclave." *New York Times*, March 30, 2010. http://www.nytimes.com/2010/04/04/travel/04journeys.html.

Fowlkes-Childs, Blair, expanded original text by Department of Ancient Near Eastern Art. "The Sasanian Empire (224–651 A.D.)." In *Heilbrunn Timeline of Art History*. New York, NY: The Metropolitan Museum of Art, 2000–. April 2016. http://www.metmuseum.org/toah/hd/sass/hd_sass.htm.

Hadingham, Evan. "Ancient Chinese Explorers." PBS, January 16, 2001. http://www.pbs.org/wgbh/nova/ancient/ancient-chinese-explorers.html.

Hansen, Valerie. *The Silk Road: A New History*. Oxford, UK: Oxford University Press, 2015.

Kuzmina, E. E. *The Prehistory of the Silk Road*. Edited by Victor H. Mair. Philadelphia, PA: University of Pennsylvania Press, 2007.

Ibn Battuta. *The Travels of Ibn Battuta in the Near East, Asia and Africa: 1325–1354*. Translated by Rev. Samuel Lee. Mineola, NY: Dover Publications Inc., 2013.

Lovell, Julia. *The Great Wall: China Against the World, 1000 BC–AD 2000*. New York, NY: Grove Press, 2006.

Maraini, Fosco, and Edward Peters. "Marco Polo." *Encyclopedia Britannica*, February 23, 2016. https://www.britannica.com/biography/Marco-Polo.

Michaelson, Carol. "Jade and the Silk Road: Trade and Tribute in the First Millennium." In *The Silk Road: Travel, Trade, War, and Faith*, edited by Susan Whitfield and Ursula Sims-Williams, 43–49. London, UK: British Library, 2004.

Millward, James. *Eurasian Crossroads: A History of Xinjiang*. New York, NY: Columbia University Press, 2009.

Quataert, Donald, and Halil İnalcık. *An Economic and Social History of the Ottoman Empire, 1300–1914*. Cambridge, UK: Cambridge University Press, 1995.

Silk Road Project. "About Us." Retrieved October 15, 2016. http://www.silkroadproject.org/about-us.

UNESCO. "Mogao Caves." Retrieved October 15, 2016. http://whc.unesco.org/en/list/440.

Wild, Oliver. "The Silk Road." Retrieved October 15, 2016. http://www.ess.uci.edu/~oliver/silk.html#5.

Wood, Frances. *The Silk Road: Two Thousand Years in the Heart of Asia*. Berkeley, CA: University of California Press, 2004.

ℐndex

Page numbers in **boldface** are illustrations. Entries in **boldface** are glossary terms.

Age of Exploration, 69, 77–80

Alexander the Great, **8**, 12–14, 46, 60
  empire of, **13**

Ardeshir I, 48–49

art, 6, 14, 42, 47, 59–63, 81

Bactria, 46

Black Death, 58–59

Buddha, **47**, **61**, 62, **63**, 64, 81

Buddhism, 6–7, 14, 19, 42, 47, 60–67, 81

Byzantine Empire, 36, 52–53, 58–59, 76

camels, domestication of, 18, 29

cannons, **75**

caravans, 4–5, **5**, 9, 11, 19, 26, 29

caravanserai, 10

Chang'an, 19, 42–43, 67

chemicals, 31, 36–37

China, 5–7, 9–12, 18–26, 32–34, 36, 38, 41–44, 47, 55–58, 60–62, 64–68, 74, 76, 79, 81
  isolationism of, 71–73

Christianity, 19, 36, 50–53, 64–68, 74, 76, 81

Colosseum, **51**

Constantinople, 51–53, 58, 74, 76

compass, 55–57

Darius the Great, 15

disease, 6, 55, 58–59, 80

domestication of animals, 18, 26–29

Dunhuang, 62

Eurasian Steppe, **25**

faravahar, **40**

Four Great Inventions, 55–56

Fujin (wind god), 14,
54, 60

Gama, Vasco da, 77–79, **78**
Genghis Khan, 21, 26,
43–46, 66
glassware, 6, **37**, 37–38
Great Schism, 52
Great Wall of China, 19,
22, **23**, 72
Greco-Buddhist art, 60–62,
81
Greece, 6, 12–14, 34,
46–47, 52, 60–62, 81
gunpowder, 6, 55–56, 80
Gutenberg, Johannes,
56–57

Han dynasty, 12, 21, 42,
48, 56, 67, 71
horses, 6, 15, 24–25, 29,
43, 48

Ibn Battuta, 44, **45**
India, 7, 13, 17, 36, 38,
43–44, 47, 60, 62,
64–65, 72, 74, 79
Islam, 7, 49–50, 53, 56–
57, 65–68, 74, 76, 81
Islamic Golden Age, 50

jade, **11**, 11–12, 36, 42
Japan, 6–7, 14, 21, 60,
62, 65, 69, 81
Judaism, 19, 67–68, 81
Justinian I, 36, 58
Justinian Plague, 58

Khotan, 11–12
Kublai Khan, 69, 71
Kushan Empire, 46, 60–62

leather, 6, 31

Ma, Yo-Yo, **82**, 82–83
Manicheans, 19, 66–67
maritime trade routes, 6,
21, 38, 56, 67, 71,
73–74, 77
middlemen, 5, 9, 20, 36
Ming dynasty, 71–73
Mogao Caves, 60, 62–63,
63
Mongols, 21, 22, 43–46,
50, 66, 69, 71
motifs, 59–60, 81
movable type, 56–57

Near East, 20, 41,
46–48, 60
New World, 17, 79

nomadic pastoralism,
26, 28
nomads, 10, 21, 25–28,
46, 48

Ottoman Empire, 53, 71,
74–76

paper, 6, 31, 38,
55–56, 80
paper money, **39**
Parthian Empire, 20,
48, 65
Polo, Marco, 4, 17, 26,
44, 46, 67, 69
precious metals and stones,
6, 31, 33, 36, 38
printing, invention of,
55–57
Protestant Reformation, 57

religion, 6–7, 14, 19, 42,
49–53, 55, 63–68, 81
Renaissance, 53, 56–57
Rome/Roman Empire, 9,
20, 34–37, 41, 47–48,
50–53, 60, 62, 65, 76
Royal Road, 15

Samarkand, 19, 44
Sasanian Empire, 48–49, 65
silk, 6, **30**, 31–36, 38,
42, 74
process of making, 33,
34, 36
Silk Road
definition of, 4–6
effects on history, 6–7,
25, 55–68, 79–81
end of, 71–79
geography of, 17–20
map of, **18**, **73**
origins of, 10
Silk Road Ensemble, **82**,
82–83
silkworms, 32–36, 44
Spice Routes, 6, 21, 73–
74, 77, 79
map of, **18**, **73**
spices, 6, 31, 38, 69, **70**,
73–74, 76–77, 79

Taklamakan Desert, 10–
11, **16**, 19, 62
Tang dynasty, 42–43, 71
Tarim Basin, 10, 12, 19,
29, 36, 67, 73

technologies, new, 6, 18,
    26–28, 55–57, 80
three hares motif, **59**,
    59–60

Umayyad Caliphate,
    49, 67

War of the Heavenly
    Horses, 21–25
wheel, invention of, 18,
    27–28
Wudi, Emperor, 21, 24–25

Xiongnu, 21–24

Yuezhi, 24, 46

Zhang Qian, 18, 24–25
Zheng He, 72, **72**
Zoroastrians, 19, 49, 66

About the Author

Derek Miller is a writer and educator from Salisbury, Maryland. His books include *Health in Contemporary Africa*; *The Economy in Contemporary Africa*; and *Earth, Sun, and Moon: Cyclic Patterns of Lunar Phases, Eclipses, and the Seasons*. When he isn't writing or teaching, Miller enjoys reading about China and the history of the Silk Road.